A STRANGER IN A FOREIGN LAND:

Memories of How it Was with a Message of Hope

By

BEN FRANK WOOD JR.

Table of Contents

Dedicated to the Loving Memory of

Peggy Coplin Wood

"Who can find a virtuous woman? for her price is far above rubies."
Proverbs 31:10

Peggy Coplin Wood finished the race and moved on to her eternal reward following a life full of loving others and pouring herself into those around her. She was the sixth of seven Coplin children born and raised in the Beech Bluff community. In 1950, she married the love of her life and they embarked on a journey together that saw them serve others in West and Middle Tennessee for several decades. After her husband, Bro Ben Wood, entered the ministry she served beside him faithfully as a pastor's wife at Laneview Baptist Church in Trenton, New Hope Baptist Church in Dyer, Tom's Creek Baptist Church in Perry County, and their final church home, Poplar Springs Baptist in Blue

Goose. She was the perfect pastor's wife and served alongside her husband in any capacity she could. Her loving nature and gentle spirit helped spread the love of Christ to everyone she came in contact with.

A loving mother, she raised a daughter and a son to love the Lord and to serve others. She always welcomed them and their friends with a smile on her face and a cold pitcher of sweet tea in the fridge. She never wanted to be in the spotlight, but she loved being around her family and friends and she saw each one as a treasure and a gift from the Lord. She never met a stranger and was usually the first one there and the last one to leave every time the church doors were open. It even happened when she visited a church where she didn't know anyone, she just loved being around God's people.

Peggy never held a high position in a company or had a corner office with a view. She worked alongside her husband as a sharecropper when they were first married, and was his partner for life in not only church work, but farming, building, beekeeping, teaching, and everything else he got them into. She never aspired to hold office or make policy, her goals were much more important. She lived her life to please Jesus, love her family, and to be an example of being content in all things.

"Who can find a virtuous woman?" Anyone who came in contact with Peggy found one.

--Prepared by Benjie Wood

Preface

In 1949 God smiled on the Ben F. Wood family and gave Ben F. Wood Jr. what he wanted to make up the Ben F. Wood Jr. family. The way he would start this family would be to bring a beautiful, mischievous, brunette into the family. From that point on the going was rough, but became a pleasure. Peggy became the better half of this new family. This family will be known as the Ben and Peggy Wood family. So the Ben F. Wood Jr. family has started with a bang.

We were married in January of 1950. We are Ben, 19 years old and Peggy, 18 years old. I am speaking as her husband now, this is "The greatest thing other than when I allowed the Lord to save me" that has ever happened to me or ever will happen.

I thought the above then, when she married me and she has never given me a chance to think any other way.

The preacher that married us had us to promise to get involved in church and we did during the first year we were married. Peggy trusted the Lord Jesus and was gloriously saved. She was baptized one cold Sunday afternoon in J.D. Stanford's pond. This made our house a home and Jesus was there through all the problems we faced and there were many as we adjusted to our new life together. He has brought us through everything that we have encountered, because we have had faith in Him. Without Him we wouldn't have made it.

In 1951 we moved to Milan, in Gibson County, Tennessee. We moved into a little three room house on a sharecrop farm, and along with making a crop I would help the landlord milk a dairy farm, and keep it going. This little house was a box house and that means the walls were one inch thick and no underpinning or insulation. Boy, did we have to fight to keep from freezing. We stayed there until we could save the money to buy our own place and that was about five years. We built a front porch on this house to make it look more like a house instead of a barn.

The temperature got down below zero while we lived there, and in the winter we would wrap the tarpaulin around our bedroom to keep the snow from blowing through the cracks and onto the bed. Our togetherness as partners, buddies, and companions would see us through, because this is what our Lord wanted for us. We worked night and day, and saved every penny we could get our hands on. In order to make extra money, I worked painting and building for the public all of the days and hours that I could leave the farm. I kept bees and would work on my bee equipment at night.

In 1956 I had gotten to where I could build houses for people and was building a house for a man that had some land for sale. So Peggy and I bought the land to put our house on. This was to be our first house of our very own. We built that first little five room house on a twenty-five acre farm. It was underpinned and insulated. I almost got killed while preparing the lot and driveway when I had a tractor accident. I had to learn to work with my left hand, and that is the way I built this house. I got the use of my arm and hand back in about one year. I was working at the gin in the day time and farming our crop by night. During that time Peggy lost a baby boy that only survived one day in this world. It was a very difficult year.

By 1957, God not only blessed me with the best wife, He now added to our family. Donna was born, and Peggy's dad died the same day she was born. Boy did we need the Lord that day. But our precious Lord saw us through that time just the same way he has seen us through all of our troubles. It seemed that we had our share of trouble during the six years that we lived there. We sold that farm in 1962 and bought some land closer to town where we built the second house. It was about this time that the Lord began really working on me to preach. We sold the farm in the fall and began building the second house, barely getting it finished when we had the worst winter we had had in a while. But the new house was insulated and warm now and we knew how to be thankful. I had to dig snow to get out of the driveway but I had to go because of the things that needed to be done.

Now the Lord was pressing me to preach and I never heard of such a thing. But I also knew that if God wanted me to preach I would have to try. I had so many excuses but I also knew that none of them would work. I kept saying, "Well, a little later."

Peggy and I both surrendered to the Gospel Ministry in 1963.

I was licensed in August 1963 by Poplar Springs Baptist Church near Milan, Tennessee. I began classes at Bethel College in McKenzie, Tennessee in September of 1963, and was called as pastor of Laneview Baptist Church at Trenton in January of 1965.

God richly blessed Peggy and I on April 22, 1967 when he added to our family a fine young man that will carry on the Ben F. Wood name, and as long as Benjie lives we will never die. Peggy and I were unable to have another baby boy after the loss of our first one, but that didn't bother our Heavenly Father. He knew what to do and handled this problem perfectly as always. We named him Ben F. Wood Jr. and the name goes on.

I pastored at Laneview six years and went straight to New Hope Baptist Church in Dyer after leaving Laneview Baptist Church in 1971. I pastored at New Hope for six and a half years and left there in 1978. In the fall of 1978 we moved to Perry County and went to Tom's Creek Baptist Church at Linden. We pastored there until 1995. Boy, what a whirl and my little wife has been in there all the while. She has been by my side all the way.

After retiring from preaching and teaching at Perry County High School, we moved back to Jackson in 1999. There I was called to pastor Poplar Springs Baptist Church at Blue Goose for about three years.

God richly blessed Peggy and me in all four of these churches.

I have worked as a builder, plumber, and electrician all the way through these ministries. I built my first house for the public in 1955 and continued to build houses for 48 years. I taught building trades at Perry County High School. And I retired as a school teacher with a teacher's pension.

I have not minded being a bi-vocational preacher, and have actually enjoyed it. After we moved to Perry County Peggy became my partner in building and worked with me on all the jobs as a fulltime hand. She and I were the only hands hired fulltime on the last house we built for the public, and part time hands were hired as needed. She worked from start to finish and didn't cull any part, from the framing with sixteen penny nails to the finish and painting work. She has been a perfect companion, through all of our ministry and business, and that includes averaging grades and filling out records for school.

In 2017 the Lord took her to Heaven to be at His side. She continues to be my strength and to, with her sweet spirit, guides me through my days. When she was preparing our tombstone in expectation of that day, she had it inscribed with the words "Together Forever" and I know that the two of us will indeed spend forever together.

Purpose

"Just remember, you are feathering your nest."

--My Father's words to his children.

There is a need to know that the things we do from the beginning, we will have to live with the rest of our life.

The Thought – The bird builds its nest, and lines it with feathers and soft things to make it more livable.

This saying of old was a reminder and warning that the choices we make and the things that are done will affect the rest of our life, and in some cases eternity.

Young people need to be reminded that they are responsible for what they choose to do with their life. They need to think: Is this what I want for the rest of my life? Is this what God wants for me?

Young people need to realize that what they choose to do presently will build their future life. There are so many things one can choose to do in the spur of the moment that they will have to deal with for the rest of their lives. The Word of God is clear on what is best for anyone in this life. A person has the ability to know God's will for his or her life.

Study the Word of God and you can be conscious of how it ought to be with your life. See Exodus 20:1-18. In the Ten Commandments the Bible tells us how it ought to be with our life. The Lord is ready to enter into a covenant with you today. See Deuteronomy 5:1-21. Verse 3 is important to us today."The Lord made not this covenant with our fathers, but with us, even us, who are all of us here alive this day."

Introduction – "We Have Come a Long Way"

Life in this world is a journey that needs direction and help. The first thing that I remember in this life is that I needed direction and training to make it here. I had God's word quoted to me very often, early, while I was very young. I heard Proverbs 22:6 quoted "Train up a child in the way he should go: and when he is old, he will not depart from it." My Dad lived by faith and therefore taught by example to direct us and by mouth to instruct us.

I only had my Dad for 13 years but he let God tell me that without what he could do in Jesus for me, I couldn't make it in this world successfully. His message is "Without Me you can do nothing" (John 15:5 NKJV). My experience has proved this to me over and over. Every time I have forgotten Him or failed to call on Him, I have failed.

I entered college as a freshman when I was 33 years old, and I still remember what the instructor told us."You cannot get an education without the Word of God." Another instructor said, "Unless you get on God's side, you will never see clearly how it is there." He said you must be born again (reference John 3:7).

When I was in public school 81 years ago I enjoyed the privilege of a real education where God was trusted each and every day. Since that day slowly but surely this society has pushed God out of the public school systems. God will not force Himself on anyone or any group, but a Godless society will ban prayer and the Ten Commandments and anything related to God from being presented to the student who has no hope without prayer and the Ten Commandments. A Godless school system has no hope without a real trust and faith in God. Without God there is no success. Any nation or school system or special interest group that cannot let God lead and direct will not succeed, for without God they can do nothing.

In 1937 I was in the first grade and our teacher took us on a field trip to Jackson. We went to Model Mills, Colonial Bakery, and the Coca-Cola plant. We got a small Coke, a little loaf of bread, and went to the picture show. After 73 years I still can see all of this, and I learned a lot that I will never forget on that day.

We began every day with Bible study and prayer, and answered the roll call with a Bible verse memorized for that time. The Lord Jesus was there to influence our tender and open hearts. He was also there to help us to learn when time came to open our other books. What the Holy Spirit helps you learn you will always remember. We knew that He was with us when test time came and we went home with the results. Today I still remember the things I learned there.

Wisdom comes from God and is the thing that helps us make decisions that we ourselves can never make. Wisdom comes to younger people when they listen to those who are older. The best classes I ever sat in were when I sat down and listened to my Dad and other older men when they shared their past experience. My Dad was a wise man and because of this when he talked, as a young boy I somehow absorbed the wisdom that was available to me. He would share experiences from his youth until his old age, and always warned me about the same mistakes he had made, not to make them. He also shared the good decisions he had made, and encouraged me there. Because of this he has guided me into the right way many times through my 88 years of life. Today I still depend on his advice. There have been many other men of wisdom in my life that I have benefited from their advice.

I might note here that there were many unwise people who were willing to offer their advice, and some of them I listened to, and I learned a lesson there also. Do not go there, and remember wisdom is of God.

One of the sad things today is that those who really know and love the Lord, are getting fewer as the days go by. So you must be VERY careful what you believe and do. Make your decision prayerfully with the Word of God.

We have come a long way and somehow gotten to the point that we have a form of godliness, but denying the power thereof. See 2 Timothy 3:1-5. Men of wisdom would say, "Got the cart before the horse" when I was a boy. We need to turn away from the deceivers and continue striving to learn from the wise. See 2 Timothy 3:14-15.

When I was nine years old our teacher in school taught us that we are a soul, and we have a body. And that God provides for spiritual needs of our soul as He also provides the needs of our body. She used some beautiful apples to demonstrate this. She took ten big red apples and lined them up on her desk in front of us and said, "God has provided these ten apples for all your needs." She set one aside, and said, "Take one of them to be used for your soul's spiritual need, and the other nine you can use for your flesh." She said that at least one tenth of what God gives us in this life should be used for the needs of man as a soul.

What we need to sustain this life we earn by working for it, and we hope to deal with later. One tenth of this should go to further the work of God in salvation and church work for the spiritual needs of man. We haven't given God anything until we have exceeded the one tenth that already belongs to God. Rightfully it all comes from Him and He reserves this one tenth in order to take care of the real needs of man, which are the needs of man as a soul.

We have come a long way, and should have learned a lot. And one thing I have learned is that Jesus has all power. I mean He is all of it. I have learned what my Dad and other wise people were talking about, and I am thankful that I listened to them. The above gave me something to think about. I considered what they had to say, and made my decision prayerfully with the Word of God. Low and behold Jesus was there all the time.

He has been there when everyone was gone. He is there when no one can do anything. His power is still sufficient when all other power is insufficient. He works when nobody else can or will work. I have found that one dollar with the blessing of God (Jesus) on it will do more than millions without God's blessings.

We are talking about getting the cart before the horse. Jesus is the only hope. He is everything. I hear unbelievers say if we spend money we do not have, we can have hope; and wonder how these people got where they are and missed my Lord. He was there when this world was created. He was there at Calvary when my salvation was bought. He was there when I was born into this world. He was there when I was saved. He has been with me all the way and will continue with me forever. He has always been there for me, and always will be....can you beat that???

When I was 13 years old, my Dad died and this was like the end of the world for me. My Dad had prepared me for that day from three years earlier. He would sit and tell me that he was getting old and would soon not be around. And that because I was the oldest I would have to step up and take the lead. He would say that he didn't have anything to leave with me materially except for the world, and that if I would work hard I would make it. He would assure me that God would make it possible, and this He did.

When I was 14, while considering what my Dad had told me before he died, I was saved. I asked Jesus to come into my heart and life. And this He did, and has been there all the way. He has been there when I got myself into trouble. He would take me by the hand, and would say 'come on now', and lead on.

When I was 14 years old, I would work for the farmers in the community when I was out of school. I would make $1.25 a day from sun up to sun down. We would gather corn and cut wood, kill hogs, whatever needed to be done. When I was 15 I farmed and traded work with the other farmers on the farm where I lived. There were very few tractors then and we farmed with horses and mules.

When I was 16 I had to quit school and go to work to help out with the family expenses. When I was 33 I passed the G.E.D. test at Bethel College and went to college there. I attended classes at Middle Tennessee State University, and at the University of Tennessee, until I was 59 years old. After that I taught high school until I retired. All this I did while pastoring a church and doing carpenter work.

When I was 16 I got my social security card and have paid in to Social Security from 1946 until 2003 and much of this as self-employment which was 15% most of the time. I remember that there was a question as to whether the Social Security program was a good idea because the government was in charge of it. Social Security was to be a retirement program, but politics has changed that in a negative way.

It has been 72 years now and I find myself in the same society where I was in 1946. We are right there because mankind has had too much to do with how he is going to survive here in this life.

I think a lot these days about how far we have come, and realize that we haven't gotten very far in following the Lord for success. Failure comes when we choose to leave God out. And this brings me to the idea that it is not good to ignore the Lord.

Part One – Life of The Stranger

Chapter 1 – Strangers in a Foreign Land

There are only two groups of people in this world as you and I know it. There are those who are born here, born of the flesh, and those who are born of the spirit, born from above.

Those who are born of the flesh must be born again. Now in the process of becoming a part of God's family they become foreigners here. This makes it necessary for them to spend their time here in this world as a stranger in a foreign land and this world is not their home, but that they are just traveling through.

If you are at home in this world, you can become pacified with the things of this world to the extent that you will never know that you are not really at home. Now this is where the Word, Christ the Lord Jesus, comes in. He will lead you through and carry you when he has to, and this is often! The weakness of the flesh cannot save anyone for flesh is the earthly part of a person, representing lusts and desires. See Ephesians 2:1-5.

The saved who are led by Jesus do not allow the world to pacify them but wholly lean on God's word. See Galatians 5:16-26.

Seventy-four years past I asked Jesus to come into my heart and life, and He did. It is these 74 years of travel in this world that I am going to account for in this writing. I wouldn't have anything to write if it wasn't for Him.

Because of the weakness of the flesh, I have nothing to brag about. There is one thing that I have learned—without Him I can do nothing. And every time I forgot or ignored Him, that is what happened. I have let Him down many times but He has been with me all the way and will be all the way to the end.

Chapter 2 – Stranger, But Not Alone

I became a stranger in this world in August of 1944 when I asked Jesus to come into my heart and live. You have to trust me here, the more you walk with Jesus the better you will understand what I am saying.

While following Jesus, He led me into the ministry as a pastor, and into college. There the first professor I had told my class that we were going to study God's word and that we would make a better grade if we were born again. He said that we would see the Word as it is when we are on God's side. Otherwise we would only hear about the Word and not really know it.

As a traveler in this world with Jesus, it is possible for us to see the real beauty of the land we travel through. The neighbors are so precious and good. It is a lonely place to be in this world without Jesus. As a teenager I began to see God caring for me in my neighbors that He used to take care of me and my family. He always had them there when we needed them. When I was a boy the neighbor looked out for children in every way. The neighbors would come together in the community, gathering with other neighbors to help anyone in need. During my teen years people followed Jesus and God's will was done. That is the effect that Heaven can have in this foreign world. No works of the flesh can ever substitute for this.

1945 was a spiritually important year, along with many other happenings that were very important. Our nation was just coming out of the second dip of a depression that came in the late 1920's with the first dip starting with the Roaring 20's when the people turned to a life in the flesh, with the lust and desires thereof and the second dip came because the nation chose to allow social leaders to tell them that the answer was in social programs and the works of the flesh, leaving God out even more."Without me you can do nothing" is what God's word says (John 15:5 NKJV). Real revival began in the early 1940s, and this is the last time this country has had real revival turning to God in complete trust.

August 14, 1945, our President announced that the war was over, and our military would be coming home. It was with excitement that reaction came. Businesses closed and people hit the streets and roads home to celebrate this answered prayer. For the last two years people had gathered at church to ask God to heal our land from this uncertainty. God had answered because His people had humbled themselves and sought His face. God's people gathered that evening to thank their Lord for victory and answered prayer. Our nation continued in revival for years to follow.

As a youth 15 years old, many things came at me from different directions. And I found that I had to make serious decisions that were important. I knew that God was leading me by His Word. And that He was at work in my heart, that I was conscious of His Will and that I must let Him lead that way. There is a saying: "Let your conscious be your guide." I have learned that accepting God means allowing Him to be your conscious.

I had learned a lot from God's word at home, at church, and at school. I am thankful that I had a home, a church, and school which had properly prepared me for my life here in this world. I was taught, by word, and by example, through the Ten Commandments and the Bible by my parents, church leaders, and my school teachers, everyday that I was there. And God helped me to listen. I am thankful that I had parents, a church, and school teachers that did their job, and God has used their faithfulness by keeping me conscious of what they taught me.

I found that at age 13, 14, and 16, I would be exposed to things that would not be best for me in this life, and would have to decide for myself what happened to me. That teaching still works today. To my regret I have not listened to that still small voice as I should have all the time.

I learned that there is another side (the wrong side) that has powerful teachers that I should not listen to or follow their example. We had among us plenty of teachers of bad things. Servicemen and women came home with plenty of teaching material, and some real bad examples, alcohol, etc.

I have had family members, church members, and classmates that had the same teaching that I have had that allowed themselves to be destroyed by the wrong teaching. Some of these were sitting with me in church the day that I went forward and asked Jesus into my heart. I had a college professor who said "You cannot get an education without the Bible." May I ask who should try? Enough said. Make sure that the education you receive can be verified in the Bible.

Chapter 3 – Strangers in a Foreign Land Lonely Without Jesus

No matter where you are you can be at home with Jesus. Without Him it is a lonely place because without Him you can do nothing. When I was 16 years of age (1946) I dropped out of school in order to help with family expenses. I was in the 11th Grade and I wanted to finish high school at a later date and it was when I was 33 years old that I was able to do something about finishing my schooling. It was 1963 that I surrendered to the ministry as a pastor and sought to finish my schooling. I was led one day to stop by a college and talk to the Dean about my education. While talking with him I mentioned wanting to come somehow and sit in classes without credit to improve my ability to study. His response was "No way. Why would you want to do that?" He then said, "We give the GED test here as an entrance test, and if you pass that I cannot keep you from coming providing you maintain a C average or better." Would you believe that Jesus and I passed that test and I went on to become a pastor and school teacher?

In 1946, my mother had married a fine man and was going to move to another county. By choice I became homeless because somehow I wanted to stay where I was. I didn't know exactly why but learned later it was because of a beautiful girl who later became my wife. I'll talk more about this later.

That fall my family moved and I moved in with a neighbor to help gather their crop and care for livestock. The next Spring I moved in with another neighbor and stayed with them for three years. I lived there until I moved in with my wife in our own home. In this time I started working in building and all kinds of painting and repair work making this my main source of income to this day.

I learned a lot when I was 16 because of the good people of God who cared for me. There are some words of wisdom for all who are tempted to choose the riches of this world over the will of God. It is better to live poorly upon the fruits of God's goodness than to live plentifully upon the products of our own sin. "Man shall not live by bread alone, but by every word that proceedeth out of the mouth of God." (Matthew 4:4 KJV)

Think about this: The bird builds its nest, and lines it with feathers and soft things to make it livable. My Dad would tell me that living in this world would be according to what I would make of it. How true to know that the things we do from the beginning we will have to live with the rest of our lives.

I have clear memories of 1935. When I was five years old, we were in a depression similar to what we were in the late 1920's. Social programs were tried that brought about "the second dip" in 1936, and following. I remember my Dad in 1935 coming home one evening saying "Enough is enough. When this week is over I am not going back." He was talking about a work program that was called W.P.A. He said that W.P.A. meant "We Piddle Around." He said that he was not going to be guilty of that, and would not be part of robbing future taxpayers of their hard earned money. He said that paying people not to work would just make things worse. And he was right, because by 1937 it was really bad. The banks went under in the mid-twenties causing Dad to lose his home and farms. The stimulus prop-ups came along and my Dad, thinking the government knew what to do, invested the rest of his money in land and built another home in 1928-1929. This he lost in 1937.

I was seven years old now, and what my Dad had said when I was five years old was right on. And from that day on I listened to what my Dad said. He thoroughly condemned government's practice of paying people not to work. I have lived 81 years since that day and have seen this happen and the results many times, and I know my Dad was right. More about this later, but I will talk about the few years until the mid-forties.

The Second Dip was the bottom and we knew it. My parents managed a cow for milk, chickens for meat and eggs, hogs for meat and lard, and a garden for meal and food. We worked there at home from sun-up to sun-down to exist.

On Thanksgiving 1937 my Dad took his gun hunting for a rabbit, squirrel, or something we could have to eat. He came back with a big woodpecker. Mother questioned eating that, but he told her that it was an Indian Chicken, and she cooked it. We had 'Chicken' and Dumplings, gravy, and broth from that bird. Dad taught me to build rabbit traps when I was nine and ten years old and we had rabbit to eat and my mother knew how to cook a rabbit. I had 21 traps and we had plenty of rabbit meat. I even sold some to my teacher and others.

There were very hard times from the mid-twenties through the thirties, and I had Christian parents and lived in a Christian community. We live in a world that hates Jesus by nature, but when one has accepted Jesus He will keep that hate from affecting you completely. This Jesus-hating world will put a wall between the parent and child when Jesus is not there to do something about it. Because of Jesus there was not a wall between me and my Dad, or separating me from any other wise person that God had there to help me. I didn't have to ask my Dad if he was a Christian because he lived it. Because of this, God used my Dad to lead me to Jesus one year after he died.

Because of this wall of separation many parents are prohibited from being what they are supposed to be to their children. The parent and the child cannot see each other, or anyone else. They are selfish by nature and cannot see beyond their own nose. Sadly we will have to talk about this later. For now let us remember that without Jesus we can do nothing.

Chapter 4 – Strangers Know Jesus Is There

Things were still hard in the mid to late 1930s and early 1940s. All this time I kept my eyes on my Dad and Mother, along with my teachers and others. As I saw their lives and their prayers, I knew Jesus was there. In August of 1944, revival had broken out in this country, and the churches were filling up. It seemed to me that everyone had come to realize that God's will was our only hope. And I knew that I needed Jesus. God had used my teacher a lot up until this point in my life, but now he used a revival that was going on in the community and it was at this revival that I was saved. He came into my heart and life and has been there ever since. I joined the church being baptized in the river along with 36 others who also were saved. The Christian people in that church helped me to grow as a new born child of God. I say this to point out that I am still growing.

Our community was typical of the nation when it came to this revival, and in our church in 1945 and 1946 the numbers were greater, our country was turning to God. Because of this revival experience people came together as a community and as a nation. When someone was sick the community was there to assist in any way they could by attending to their every need. The love of God was seen in and through the people by what they allowed the Lord to do through them. Yes, Jesus walked the dark hills and lighted the way.

We were truly in a survival mode. We worked together as a community and nation to accomplish this as we followed our Lord. God's people came to help gather our crops, cut our wood, and everything that needed to be done. We had to have wood to cook our meals and heat our homes and everyone watched to see if his neighbor needed help in any way. Everyone watched to see if they could help with the neighbor's crop. The community school was run by a united community. The women would get together to can produce for the school when the gardens were ready to gather. The women would take turns cooking at the school. Wood was cut for the school's cooking and heating by the men of the community. The community would take a bail of cotton and get together and make mattresses. They would get together at the school building and work on the mattresses. The people would get together on Saturday night and have Country music. They would get together once and a while for a barbecue and cook-out. This was done in a loving spirit of unity.

1947 brought on more of the same, and Jesus was permitted to work in our community and nation every day. It was hard but a growing experience for me. We had to have hard times to be able to appreciate God's blessings. These hard times have made it possible for me to appreciate His blessings in and for my life. God permits hard times to happen so He can enable us to know firsthand what He can and will do for us.

When I was 17 years old, in 1947, I joined the National Guard. It was the Tennessee Guard at that time but became the National Guard at a later date. We would meet once a week for drill and training. We had Chapel one night and our Chaplin brought the message. I was just a teenager then and ordinarily I would not pay that much attention to what was being said. But somehow the Lord caused me to hear and remember what was said in that message. He made a statement that has affected my entire life since that day.

The message was about the danger of leaving God out of our lives individually and nationally. He reminded us of the fear that our country had of the dangers of Communism and how it would come to take over and destroy our nation. Communism is a word that is used to describe when man has taken matters into his own hands to try to provide for himself the things that only God can provide. These are social programs that man thinks that he can provide for himself, and that God cannot be trusted to do. Jesus says that without Him we can do nothing. It is all about God's will and way, completely.

As a communist nation Russia and the Soviet Union proceeded to take over other nations and seek to supply them with their needs for development and literally everything. The Soviet Union failed, and we were told that they would, because they left God out. Our preacher said that the main leader of Russia had said that America would turn her back on the Lord and turn to Communism. He explained that America had turned to God and that He was going to bless the nation abundantly with all the material things that would come, and that money would become the God of this great nation. She would forget God and like other nations turn to Communism.

It has been 71 years and with this message in mind, I have watched this great country, great because of God, gradually turn her back on Jesus, and turn to the things of the flesh which cannot satisfy the real needs of man and will not please God. In creation, God breathed into man and he became a living soul. God gave man a part of himself, which makes a spirit (soul) who has a body. The primary need of man is spiritual, and in Jesus, God has made it possible. In this world mankind is born in the flesh and the needs of the flesh are provided. Man has a responsibility to the flesh, but his first and greatest need is spiritual and must be met at all costs for the benefit of the soul and body in that order.

Seek first the kingdom of God, His righteousness, and God will make it possible to provide for the needs of the flesh. Try Him.

Man is a partner with God here and God wants him to work for his living, and earn the needs of the flesh. The way of our Lord is work to help others and God will help us. We are all in this together and need each other in order for God to bless spiritually and materially.

We live in this world and love Jesus with all we are and have, and our neighbor as much as our self. When you get to this point in life you are getting somewhere. Remember now, the love of money and material things is the root of all evil, but we must love the Lord our God with all we are and have. And our problems socially will be solved here in this world, and the Communist will have to go somewhere else. Praise the Lord.

The rest of this writing will be about the encounters I have had with this nation turning its back on God. Every day that I have lived in this world I have become more of a stranger here.

Chapter 5 – Strangers Led Who Listen to God

In 1948 and 1949 I worked on a farm and trapped for mink in the Walker Bottom next to the farm where I lived and worked. Things economically were picking up and our nation had a new leader that had led us away from many of the social programs that had made it hard on small businesses. But many of these programs still exist today.

These years that I simply worked to exist and have a temporary home, things seemed to move economically and this made me want to begin to make a life for myself. I became dissatisfied with where I was in life. At this point in my life a beautiful girl came into my life and this changed my outlook on life for the better. On January 7, 1950 she became my wife and now I had a partner to face life in this world. We rented a farm and began farming, carpentering, and painting to make a living. We had a little check from the National Guard to help us with this.

After this first year we moved to another county to help run a dairy and milk cows. We lived on this farm and made a crop, along with the construction work. While here my wife and I decided to save our money to make a down payment on our own farm home. This we did, and it was hard on both of us. We worked at this place about five years and lost a baby boy in this time to add to the hard times we had there.

God was blessing our country and things were picking up economically, and I was able to build the first two houses for the public as a contractor. This was a boost for us and things were looking better.

We had the most adverse weather while we lived on this farm in the mid fifties. It was the coldest winters and hottest summers that my wife and I had to endure. We lived in a house that was like a corn crib, not underpinned, no insulation. We had our love, and the Lord to keep us warm. We worked night and day, in order to save money to have a home where we could have a better life with insulation and water with a bath in the house. It was in the mid fifties that we had our first water in the house. And we are thankful for it to this day. While we were on this farm we would raise a crop of cotton and go to town and get hands to pick it. I would go early in the morning and drive through the street of the town until I had a load of people to pick cotton that day. As I drove down the street, the people would come out with their cotton sack and get on the truck. In the fall of 1955, my wife and I raised the cotton and when we went to find hands to work, we didn't find any willing to work. They explained that they were getting a government check and if they worked and made money they would lose their check. So that put a stop to that for my wife and me and for many other struggling farmers.

In 1956 we bought a small farm and began to make plans to build our first home there. While preparing a place and driveway for the house, my tractor reared up and fell back on me. That could have been the last of me, but the Lord had a friend there with his tractor to clear the tractor off of me and carry me to the hospital, saving my life. Our friends came to the hospital to offer their help and handed my precious wife the money to pay my hospital and doctor bills. Our friends were there to let Jesus use them. God worked in the complete healing of my body. In the fall of that year I built our little house and we moved into it that winter. The house wasn't finished but what was finished was warm and cozy. That was the year that there was a recession in our nation, but for some reason the leaders didn't interfere with it and the people worked it out. The thing that hurt the most was the housing industry.

But that only helped my wife and I for we had saved the money that we needed to go as far as we did. We learned that what Dad had said 'to save the money for what you want and then it will be all yours' was right in more ways than one. We picked up bargains and were able to get more house for the money. This recession did not become a depression because the leaders didn't try to fix it, and let the people work it out. With the help of the Lord this great country can come out of anything.

1956 was a hard year for us because it was the time that so much happened to us. We lost a little boy at birth. The tractor accident happened and it was the year that was so hot in the summer. But we were still able to build our house, move in, and settle into our first home that we owned. We knew how to be thankful because we had never had a house that good.

1953 and following we had a little recession, but it didn't hurt too much because the people worked this out very well. The leaders gave the people that were picking cotton a welfare check and they couldn't pick cotton because they would lose their check. So that shut down the hand picking of the cotton. Machine picked cotton became the way in 1956, and following. The Korean War was over and people left Milan in droves to find work. The Army Ammunition Plant practically shut down. Many of the people went to the Red Stone Arsenal in Alabama. Needless to say the construction work in Milan was about shutdown because of this. The Lord took care of us, and I went to work at a cotton gin, building a new building and upgrading the machinery. And I wound up ginning cotton for about five years until construction picked up. That was dirty hard work, but we could live on that. My wife delivered us a beautiful little girl at this time, and she is a blessing to us.

It was while working at the gin that I purchased us a new Chevrolet truck, our first new vehicle, and boy were we proud. All these things happened while we were working through a recession. That is what the Lord can do when you trust Him. He surely has brought my wife and me a long way in those first ten years.

Chapter 6 – There Is a Need to Be Alert

When passing through the world as a stranger, there is a need to be aware of where we are. The Bible gives us the road signs to let us know where we are in this life on the earth and lets us know how to react to where we are and what we are doing. If we are alert we will react to the signs that we see along the way in the Bible. These signs are the posted way for us to react at that time and place. When we travel today the roads we travel have signs to tell us where we are going and how to get there, how to stay on the right road, how fast to go at that point, when to stop and yield to others who are travelers here and dangers that we will encounter, and when we are nearing our destination. The Bible serves as our signs.

Any person who has become a stranger and is living in this world is simply passing through. We have a road map and posted signs in the Bible, and must use them in order to be aware of the presence of Jesus and His leadership protection, because He says "Without me you can do nothing."

This chapter we hope will help anyone who has become a true stranger, and is simply passing through to be alert to God's way to pass through this life properly.

While traveling (living life here) we need to pay attention to where we are in this life. This we are able to do by using the Word of God. At all times, by this we know where we are in our life (journey) and where we are going. Over the years in my life here I have noticed that we have a way of bolting through this life without ever taking time to think about where we are and where we are going. We have come a long way here, but not in the right way. When I was a boy in public school, education always contained the Word of God. Those who are wise today will tell you that without the Word of God you cannot get an education. Where would I be today if I hadn't had a family, a church, and a school that knew that I needed a real education above all of my other needs? Because I believe the Word of God I know that there are teachers who are teaching our future generations today that the Word of God is not important, and that there is no need to pay attention to God. You can start with the Garden of Eden and study History up to today and you will know where this comes from. Travel today would be impossible if we ignored the posted signs and directions along the roadways, and the Word of God teaches us that without a vision the people perish. The Word of God is the light. Use it and see.

There has been a constant effort over the eighty-eight years that I have lived in this world, by the family, the church, and the educational system to leave the Word of God out of life here. We have gotten to a point that when we are honest with ourselves we wonder why we should go to church, or school. This can happen when we do not care what God says. At home, if we care what God's will is for our lives, we will hunger and thirst for it and will do everything we can to find and know His Will for our lives. We will surely be blessed when we do.

At this point I am going to reveal some of the things that I have witnessed that have led us to think that God's will is not important in this life. I have actually been told that it is all right to study the Word of God, but don't take it too seriously. I have been told that I am a Bible worshipper, and that this is not good. I have been told the Bible is not actually the Word of God. We could go on and on with what we have been told, but we need to talk about what is more powerful here. I want to tell you about my parents and family, my church, and my school. My parents didn't get to attend school very long. But they knew the Word of God, and taught and were taught by examples. They very seldom read the Bible to us, but they lived it and we could not miss that.

When I was a boy, our church assisted in our worshiping and serving the Lord and actually made it possible for us to assist in the ministry of Jesus in the salvation of the lost. The church made up of human beings was the body of Jesus here on the earth and through His body (the church) He can take care of all the needs of mankind. Because of this the church has the only hope and love for mankind.

When I was a boy, the church was called God's House, and I knew it when I went there. There was enough respect for God that He was felt by all that entered His presence. There was no way that a lost person could enter without being convicted of their lost condition. Therefore many repented and turned to Jesus for salvation. There was no way that those who were born again (saved) could be there without being miserable, because God would help His child to grow spiritually.

When I was a boy, the structure, or building, no matter how humble, was dedicated to God. It was His on the earth for His purpose. Sometimes it was a brush arbor or a majestic temple. Because it was God's, those who respected God were blessed and grew spiritually there.

When I was a boy, it was at church that I learned respect for God. The church is a partner with the family in teaching respect for God and His Word. On Calvary Jesus paid for the salvation of the lost and left His church here to minister and teach respect for God and His Word. The most important building in the community is God's House and the most important body of people in the world meets there. God adds to

His church (His body) all who are born again. What does the church mean to you?

When I was a boy, it was at public school that I learned to read the Bible. The school was a partner with my parents and the church in teaching me to respect and read the Word of God and to respect Him.

God will bless anyone who is alert and respects Him and His Word. Just think of the many that do not have and show respect for Him and His Word. We have come a long way from respecting God's word as a family, and as a church, and as the educational system.

I know that 88 years ago there was more respect for God and His Word, and it was seen in the lives of the family, the life of the church, and the school, the educational system. There is a great need to be alert to the Will of God.

Now we know that it is not impossible for us to go back to the time when as a whole we have more respect for God and His Will. We have families today that are alert to God and His Word. We have scriptural churches today that respect God and His Will. We have schools today that are assisting the families and churches in teaching God's will for this life. The old song goes "The Lord still walks the dark hills" to light the way. The Lord is still in these schools and can be seen in the progress of the students. Until this day, wise teachers have said that no one can get an education without God.

The early history of this country is that education is a product of the church. Give God the credit. Education is the arm of the church and is used in its mission work, both local and foreign; to teach people to read and prepare them to carry out God's will for their lives. From our early history until now the families always had the local church doubled as a school or had a building nearby to complete the community needs. The families of the community had the church, and the school to carry the commission of Jesus, to teach all nations, and teach them to observe the will of God. Now Christ made a promise to be with them to give them success. So we still have schools today that are doing this.

Chapter 7 – The Primary Need of Man, From a Stranger's Point of View

Man is more than flesh. He is a spirit, because God created man as a spiritual being. God breathed into man the breath of life, and this made Him a living soul, who has a body of flesh. Flesh is the dwelling of the soul here on earth. Mankind is a little world, consisting of Heaven and earth, soul and body. For man to live here on the earth, he must have a body of earth, as a spiritual being. The soul is the real human, noble and excellent, who has a body of flesh that is a worthless useless carcass, apart from the soul. The flesh is the enemy of the spirit (soul) with only one purpose, the dwelling place of the soul. Flesh represents the lust and desires, and is contrary to the spirit. When the soul moves out the body is worthless and goes back to the earth.

As a stranger in a foreign land we find that our writing here is about a person who repented and has asked Jesus to come into their life and is born again. So a stranger is a living soul who has an earthly dwelling place. The danger for a person originally born in the flesh is to live as if the worthless flesh is all of it, and that Jesus died on the cross in vain. The stranger in a foreign land has a different story to tell.

Jesus, the Christ, was a good example of a person who is saved and in this world. We must realize that a dual nature exists now and we must live accordingly. God has honored mankind with the freedom to choose right from wrong. To know if we choose right or wrong is determined by God's will for our lives. We have God's will revealed for us in His Word. The 'Ten Commandments' are an example, revealing how it ought to be. This is the only way we can know if we are right or wrong. God's word tells us that righteousness is of God. So we see that respect for God and His Word will cause us to be right.

When we are saved the battle is on, and Jesus will lead us to victory when we want to be right. The Word tells us to seek first the kingdom of God and His righteousness and we will not be wrong.

God's word tells us that we have to take charge and be right. That as a living soul we must take charge in order for God's will to be done in our lives, for the flesh is contrary to the spirit and will always lead us to be wrong. The flesh has desires and lusts after them. That is not the will of God for us.

Having a dual nature, we have a responsibility in this life to let our right nature reign. The old Indian said, "It is like a man has two hunting dogs in him, and the one that he calls on will go." Where does the decision we make come from? There was a saying that my parents and other wise people would say when I was growing up, that went like this, "What in Heaven's sake are you doing?" They would use this when they wanted me to recognize whether I was right or wrong. Jesus would say "Let him deny himself and take up his cross and follow me." (Matthew 16:24) The Bible teaches that the things that we would do naturally we cannot do.

When we invite Jesus into our life, He brings the power for us to choose that that will please God over the power that will not please Him. So you see we have in Jesus all that is necessary for God's Will to be done. It is in the righteousness of Jesus that we are able to choose to be right with God, and not in what we are able to do. Our righteousness is no good, because the flesh cannot satisfy God's Will. The spiritual side of us is able, but the flesh is not.

Now I have shared what I have observed in this life from 1944 until now 2018. Our civilization has progressively turned to the flesh and we are in trouble because of this. Now remember that there are still churches and people that live by and for God.

The flesh will take over when permitted. The things of the flesh are not the primary need of man, but there are real responsibilities to take care of the bodies properly. Our health is necessary for us to carry out God's will in this life. God is our helper in the needs of our bodies. It is wrong for us to mistreat our bodies and fail in God's will for them. Because man is a living soul he must have a body and that body is important in life here on earth.

The fact that man is a spiritual being and that God has plans for mankind makes it necessary for man to realize that as a soul God's word is the only way.

It is easy for people to care about the needs of the flesh. This is good and God expects this of us, but if we neglect the greater need we have failed in God's Will for our lives. The greater need of mankind is his primary need. God's word tells us that if we gain the whole world and lose our soul we have failed. Some have said "Feed the body and starve the soul." You have failed in the greater need of man. Much of our society caters to the needs and pleasures of the flesh. But there are still many who have their priorities right. So we are able to see that it can be done.

Chapter 8 – The Things of the World and How We Are Tempted to Them

The things of this world are temporal and only last for a while. Because of this we need to pay attention to what we look for in this life. What will do in the long run? When we are through with these bodies, they will go back to the earth. And then what will we have? We are to look for only that that will last.

The things of this world will not last and for those who try to love and depend on them will fail to have satisfaction. This we can know if we pay attention as we pass through this life. When I was 17 years old and was in the National Guard, we drilled once a week, and trained as soldiers. One evening our chaplain preached to us for chapel. And the message I heard has never left me. His message was that man can turn his back on God. In 1947 our country was in real revival. We had experienced depression economically and world wars and gone to our knees in prayer and God had blessed us. Our chaplain told us that God would bless America because of this and she would turn her back on God. He was referring to what was called Communism that we had been warned about in Grade School. In a communist state the people trust in and love temporal things and do not trust in God. They don't really trust God and love Him, and somehow I have allowed God to keep me remembering this message. During my lifetime since that day I have watched our great nation do exactly what this message said and leave God out.

God has blessed our nation in my lifetime to an extent that it is hard to believe and if I hadn't seen it I wouldn't believe how we have been blessed. Our nation has been a blessing to the whole world because of her faith in God. We must never forget that this is only the temporal needs and our greater needs are the treasure we are to lay up in Heaven. The spiritual needs, we must remember along with our temporal needs are the most important needs. Our spiritual needs are the work of Jesus, our Lord who says "without me you can do nothing."

Our comfort, peace, and wellbeing, history (His 'story') reveals this, and there is no history without Jesus. The world was built by and around Him, and without Him would not exist.

In college I studied the History of Civilization, and in the study all nations that left God out, as America has, ceased to exist in history. Now there are families, churches, and schools that have not left God out, but those who are leaving God out of their existence are all about 'us.'

The Word of God tells us that we cannot serve two masters. Choose to serve God every day. We must love God with all that we are and have, and we will love our neighbor as our self. Now we have our life on track and God is at work. We make a conscious effort to put God first and live. This is called a commitment, dedication and being right with God. It is because we have another love. This puts temporal things where we do not worship them.

When God is at work we will not fulfill the 'lust' of the flesh. (See Galatians 5:15-26) But will bear the fruits of the spirit. Our nation is in trouble right now, and it seems that our leaders just don't get it. It seems that they have somehow been educated without ever coming to knowledge of the truth, where Jesus says "without me you can do nothing." This nation has been a great nation because our forefathers had love for and faith in God. Only God can make a nation great.

We need to know there is the right way and there is a wrong way. There has to be a wrong way in order for there to be a right way. We need to understand what is wrong before we can turn to the right, because the battle is with powers of this world, see Ephesians 6:12.

God is so important that when He is left out, failure is guaranteed. God will let us fail when we want to. Remember that when we live in the flesh and this world only, we are condemned already. God in His Son Jesus has bought our salvation and success and it is not of the works of the flesh or this world.

We have to ask ourselves here where we have gone wrong? We have allowed the devil to use the blessings of God against us. Just think of the technology, machinery, conveniences that God has blessed us with. Look at technology, television, internet, and cell phones. The television has been used to brainwash and destroy young people by the millions. The devil and his powers will use all this against us if we do not wake up and teach and warn for the right.

We have allowed the 'rulers of darkness' to use technology and get away with it long enough. Our society as a whole is being destroyed by the rulers of the air. There are people of all ages that have allowed themselves to be destroyed by technology that is basically good. There are youth that are in jail with their lives ruined who were trapped by the misuse of texting, etc. There are people of all ages in jail because of the misuse of technology.

Young people have been influenced and had their lives ruined and destroyed because of our failures as a nation in leaving God out of our lives. We have not taught our youth what the devil is doing and that there is right and wrong. Remember there will be some that will listen to the message and will allow the destroyer to destroy them. But many will listen and will be delivered.

Some may say "what can we do?" Well, we can do what many are doing today. Families are teaching God's word. Most of all, they are living it as examples. That is what families were doing when I was a boy 80 years ago. There are also churches that are scriptural churches that are teaching God's word and living it as an example. That is what they were doing when I was a boy. Also there are successful schools today that are teaching the word of God and living it as examples. All of the above are being done so that in the future America may be great.

You can ask the Godly family, scriptural church, and the Godly school system what they think about God's work and the Ten Commandments, and they will tell you they are important and very necessary, and will tell you about Jesus.

Be reminded that if you as a family live God's word, the devil will get mad. If your church is a scriptural church it makes the devil mad. And if your school system teaches God's word, the Ten Commandments and Jesus, the devil is mad.

The Word of God tells us to act under the influence of the blessed spirit. Then we will not allow our corrupt nature to fulfill the lust thereof. The spirit will use the word to make known to us the will of God.

We are told by the word of God that when we bite one and another, and are consumed one of another, that we need to act (walk) by the spirit, and not fulfill the lust of the flesh. See Galatians 5:15-16.

Now our chaplain said that when America leaves God out that she will in fact be destroying herself from within and in this vacuum will elect people who will try to supply the needs of man without ever thinking that God alone is the way man's needs are met. Mankind will come to the place where he will not know that the flesh profits nothing.

Beware of the condition where man will not allow God in his thinking, and will try to take care of himself. America is not there yet, but we see the signs all around that we are getting close. There are still many families, churches, and schools that teach by example that there is a God who is man's greatest need.

Chapter 9 – Darkness and Enlightenment, What is It?

God's word, the Bible, is a lamp to enlightenment. And without it man dwells in darkness. Darkness symbolizes error, evil, and the work of Satan. When a person is born into this world, they are born into darkness and must have the light to see their way out and through this world.

A look at history and the dark ages through which mankind has had to pass in order to fulfill God's purpose for him here in this world, called for him to be enlightened with light from above. Now that light from above is Jesus, God's Son. He is that life that God wanted mankind to have, and that life became the light of men.

Without a light a person cannot see in darkness, and the lack of light makes vision impossible. And God's word says that "Where there is no vision, the people perish" (Proverbs 29:18) and there is no happiness. This can only come by being enlightened, and that is by Jesus who is the light of mankind.

When I was a boy, I had parents, a church, and a school, that held the light and lighted the way for me. They didn't shine it in my eyes and blind me with it. They never walked in the darkness and tried to use God's word to correct me. They held the word and lighted the way for me.

Jesus has a question for us. Should we light a candle to put it under a bushel and try to hide it? (Mark 4:21) He says no, we are to let our light shine so everyone is able to see God's good work, and give Him the glory.

In my lifetime I have watched those who love the darkness try to take away the light so the darkness will not be destroyed. Prayer is the most important 'light' that I saw and learned. I learned from my parents as they walked in the light of prayer and held me a light here. My church was the house of prayer. Every time we gathered as a church a light was held so I could be enlightened in the way, and this light never let me down. My school teachers never allowed anyone or anything to keep them from holding the light so I could be enlightened regarding prayer. I watched while we allowed those who love the darkness to tell us that we couldn't have prayer in the public school. As a public school teacher I wondered how anyone, not even the devil, could keep me from praying, and because I had been enlightened I prayed more in school after that. And because of Jesus, prayer became easier and more often. I seems to me that they do not to know what prayer really is and how much we need to gather for prayer.

It is a great privilege for any family to have God's house in the community as the house of prayer where God's family here on earth can get together to talk with God and express our needs collectively. The Bible says that when two or three agree on earth that God will hear and answer according to our needs (Matthew 18:19). The church is the body of Jesus here on earth, and Jesus has all power to take care of our needs.

When it comes to enlightenment and the awful thought of not having it or allowing it to be kept from us, it makes me very sad today that many have lost the value of God's house in this life. In my early years in this life when the real estate agents advertised a home in the community the main selling point was that there was a church and a school in the community. As a boy I learned to pray from my parents, my church, and at my school. When my parents taught me the need of prayer in my life it reinforced the teaching of the church, and then my school teaching was in full support of the teaching of my family and church.

There is a great need for a child of God to communicate with their family in heaven. The way I see it we have allowed the works of darkness to interfere with this privilege while we are in this world. It is the greatest need for those who are away from home.

When I was called on to be away from home for a period of time, it was the greatest thing to be able to read a letter from home. God has given us in the Bible, a letter that cannot be substituted when we understand that God wants to tell us something. God wants us also to call home regularly to communicate with Him. Many of God's children allow themselves to be negligent in prayer, and this is not God's will because He wants us to recognize what He does for us. We are able to know that the Lord is our shepherd and we do not have to want. Jesus says that we have not, because we ask not (James 4:2).

The power of darkness doesn't want us to pray, because when we pray the devil has to run because error, evil, and the works of Satan are defeated. When it comes to prayer there are many families, churches, and schools that still know the value of faith and real prayer. What can I say; we still can have God's will here.

As I grew up (passing through this world) I saw clearly that the powers of darkness were making an effort to do away with the effectiveness of God's precious word. At this point this was being done by trying to hide the way that God says things morally should be when His will is fully done. God gave us the Ten Commandments so we can make a judgment as to where we are right or wrong.

Why on earth would educated people want to do all that they can do to prevent our children from knowing right from wrong? I know that the Bible teaches us that we must have and hear the message of the Old Testament before we can turn to Jesus. There have been many faithful preachers who have stood with the truth that unless we hear the message of Moses and the prophets we cannot turn to one that was raised from the dead. The old preachers would say, "Sic Moses on them." That means be sure that you make the Ten Commandments available to them. Then they will have an idea how it should be. The Bible teaches that without a vision the people perish. (Proverbs 29:18) Any one will have trouble knowing how lost they are if they do not have the Ten Commandments to reveal this to them. Jesus said that He did not come to destroy God's standard for our living, but fulfill it completely. (Matthew 5:17-20) And this He did and He only could do.

It has been alarming how our nation and the world have ignored the will of God for mankind's living over the period of my life time. When I was a boy 80 years ago, it was a daily experience for me to hear about how God said it ought to be in my living here in this life. I was told and showed how to improve. This was done by having reference to the Ten Commandments as God's standard for living.

The attacks have come in many ways on the Ten Commandments. The fact they are being removed from display in our public schools is an effort to keep our children from knowing right from wrong and to keep them from knowing what God's will is for their living here on this earth. In history (Old Testament) we find nations that tried to live without God's will, failed and fell, and that is still true today. God's will is not impossible now, because there are families, churches, and schools that still live with God's will and still teach the Ten Commandments.

When it comes to the darkness of evil and the need for enlightenment, it amazes me how intelligent people could leave God's word out when it comes to justice in this world. Not only have we sat by and watched while those in authority have banned the Ten Commandments from our schools and even some churches, but courthouses as well. Where have these judges come from?

Mock trials have become a way of life in many of our justice systems, simply because we have left the Ten Commandments out of life. Man continues to make decisions without considering God's will.

Chapter 10 – Death and Judgment

God's word wants man to know that he or she has an appointment with death and then judgment. It is a fact that a person is born into this world, and the only way out is by death. Now we are talking about being born in the flesh. To be born in the flesh is born of this world. Meaning that man in the flesh is no more than clay and will eventually go back to the earth. Because of this by the flesh a person can accomplish nothing. Flesh is the tabernacle that man has to have to exist in this world, or life. In creation God formed man out of the clay of the earth, and breathed into him the "Breath of Life" and he became a living soul. (Genesis 2:7) Man is more than flesh or body. Therefore a person must deal with this body and take care of it for God's will to be done here.

A person is more than flesh or "clay" that will go back to the earth. This person is really supposed to go to a place where spiritual beings are suited for, and this is why he is a stranger here in this world. To be absent from the body is to be present with the Lord, so a person must be born again, born from above. (2 Corinthians 5:8) Because when one is born into this world in the flesh, dead in trespasses, they must be born spiritually. Here is where Jesus comes in as Saviour.

Simply put, to be born only in the flesh is to be born into trespasses and sin, and we must be born again spiritually. We must realize that God in His word teaches that to be born as a worldly being makes it necessary for us to be born into God's family. Now this is done by believing that God sent His Son to save those in this world who wanted to be saved and not perish as a worldly being. Everyone must ask Jesus to come into their life and depend upon Him to stay there to make eternal life possible.

Now God's word tells us that there will be a day of resurrection when all who have accepted Jesus as their Saviour will be called out of the graves and this world to be with the Lord forever. Now those who have not been born again will also be called forth out of the graves and the world to stand before God in the judgment. These will be hopelessly lost forever. Only those who have truly trusted Jesus will be with the Lord from there on. Be sure to know that God and God only will be the judge at that time. This is not what some may think.

Remember that Jesus makes the difference and without Him you can do nothing. I have experienced how much the attitude of man toward God has changed over the years. Because of this a person will gradually miss the truth and fail. The fact that a person has an appointment with death and then the judgment is a message that everyone must hear and understand. This brings me to a message that I received as a young boy very loud and clear."Blessed are the dead that die in the Lord." (Revelation 14:13) This brings hope to those who have believed and put their trust in Jesus.

As a boy the message of the resurrection of the believer and the judgment of the unbeliever was seen and heard. This message was the topic of the family, the church, and the school, and we couldn't miss it. When we visited or passed the graveyard we were reminded of this message. The message is that Jesus will appear in the eastern sky, suddenly, to bring about the resurrection of the believer who died in the Lord, and the judgment of the unbeliever. This would be a sudden, unannounced experience "as the lightening cometh out of the east" (Matthew 24:27 KJV) flashes across the entire sky. The majority of graveyards in my boyhood days had the graves of the dead lying east and west, so that the resurrected soul when raised up would be facing the east. Now what was the message here?

Those in Christ who truly believe that in Jesus there is resurrected life after death are ready, ready in Jesus for the day of resurrection and the judgment to follow. No one can know when this day will come. There is no message more important than this in 1 Thessalonians 4:13-17. As a pastor of small country churches, I have stood at the head of hundreds of graves facing the east to bring comfort and hope to loved ones with this message of God.

When you pass the graveyard think about this message. Are you ready for the resurrection? Are you ready for the judgment? God's word has assured everyone that they have a sure appointment with death and after this the judgment. (Hebrews 9:27)

Now before you pass judgment on those communities that oriented their graves to face the east, prayerfully study God's word. A good scripture passage to study is Matthew 24. Listen to Jesus.

Chapter 11 – The Stranger Here on Earth Will Never Get Out of the Reach of God

Those who have come to Jesus for redemption and are saved will never get out of the reach of God while passing through this earth. It is possible to become negligent and ignore God's word and find ourselves in disrespect for God's will for our lives here in the earth. This puts us in deep trouble but never out of the reach of the love of God. The grace of God is sufficient in our salvation, redemption, and security, of all who come to Jesus and ask Him to come into their lives. When we find ourselves in error of what God wants we can allow Jesus to take us by the hand and lead us back to where God wants us.

Your best friend will fail you, but not Jesus. He is always ready to rescue you from any mistake you have made because of any negligence of respect for God's word. He will take you by the hand and lead you back into God's will for your life. When our relationship with God is broken we are lonely and miserable until we are back in fellowship with our precious Heavenly Father. Nothing is any better for the child here on earth than to be in full fellowship with our Heavenly Father.

The Bible God gave us is the rulebook for His family, and this is the way to understand what God's will is. God gives plenty of room for improvement here for the best of us. God deals with us all equally. God gave us the Ten Commandments as a list of what it would take to perfectly fulfill His will for mankind. Now it is impossible for man in the flesh to claim to be able to keep all that is in this list. The Bible as the word of God tells us the way it is to be done. Only Jesus can keep all that is necessary for God to be pleased. Jesus came not to destroy anything on this list but to fulfill it perfectly. And only in Jesus can anyone have full fellowship with God. "Without me you can do nothing" (John 15:5 NKJV) is the message Jesus has for the child of God while here on earth.

Now the Ten Commandments are the only way anyone can know right from wrong! Those who think they can know right from wrong any other way actually confuse each other, and arguing begins that never comes to a satisfactory conclusion. God's word is to be accepted or rejected, and is not up for debate. God doesn't need man's fleshly intelligence.

The born again believer loves the Ten Commandments because they love their Father in Heaven. Those who hate the Father will hate His word. This is one of the most astonishing things that I have witnessed in my 80 years as a child of God in this world. How can a child of God not be hurt deeply by the hatred that is going on in this society, in its treatment of the Ten Commandments and God's word as a whole? The natural thing for those who love God is to love His word. Dear Friend, do not join the choir and try to sing "Oh How I Love Jesus" if you do not love and respect His word. (See John 14:21)

When I was a boy the church and the school in the community that I lived in assisted my family in the teaching of right from wrong, by teaching the word and the Ten Commandments. Eighty years later I find myself in a society where you have to look hard to find a church that teaches right from wrong by teaching the Ten Commandments and the public schools do not care. They now hide the Ten Commandments from the children.

When I was a boy 80 years ago, the churches and school systems were what I call scriptural (meaning they were based on the Word of God). The Ten Commandments were referred to as the Law, and known as our schoolmaster that would bring us to Jesus Christ.

The Word of God is sufficient for the salvation of all mankind (Luke 16:31). We have Moses and the Prophets, Christ and the Apostles. Here we have God's complete way of salvation, and man cannot come to God any other way but by Jesus. Christianity is a way of life, for all who are saved.

It is amazing how religion as a whole has affected Christianity in my lifetime as a child of God here in this life. Religion is a way of worship. Man can worship anything. Denominations are congregations that have their own specific beliefs and practices of worship so to speak. Christianity is a way of worship, a philosophy—the lover of wisdom. When one is born of the spirit Jesus has come into their life. They begin to hunger and thirst for God's word. One of the most popular songs in my younger days was "Give Me That Old-time Religion," referring to the philosophy of Christianity, (the old-time way of worship). Secular philosophies such as humanism, communist materialism, and capitalist materialism will affect the minds of real Christians if they are not guarded. This is done with spiritual weapons (2 Corinthians 10:4-5). I watched as a boy and young man as denominations of religions argued that their way of worship was correct, wasting time until they didn't have time to serve the Lord. I told a sincere person once that while we were wasting time debating, people are going to hell.

Chapter 12 – Respect for Parents and Those who are Older than Ourselves

One of the things that I saw in my life here was how young people failed to have respect for their parents and those who were older than themselves. The reason for God to want them to honor their parents and those who were older was the teaching process he had planned for mankind. God clearly placed the responsibility on the parent and the older people to bring up the child in the right way. And the youth should respect the parent and older person as such.

There is a need for discipline here because this world and the flesh will lead in the wrong direction. God's Word (His Will) and faith in Jesus will bring the parent and older person to fulfill their duty here, and bring up the child in the way of God. God will always work in those who have faith here to make them successful. He will always work in those who will honor His Will here. He has a special promise to those that honor their parents and those who are their teachers that they will have a longer life, with His blessings here. So when God's will is done the parents do the Will of God and the child learns God's way for them. So when we honor God's will by honoring our parents and teachers, all will be well with us.

My life here in this world has been a pilgrimage with Jesus and many times I have been influenced by this strange world, but Jesus has been there all the time. Now I say this to say that this world will not help anyone when it comes to honor where honor is due. First you must come to Jesus if you are redeemed from this world. Then and only then can you expect God's will to be done in your life here.

There are many people who have had godly parents and teachers, who have lived this life influenced by the wicked world, that have at the last come to Jesus because of those godly parents and teachers when they have honored them at the last. When parents and teachers have been used to bring up a child, that child will not get away from their teaching. I have witnessed many times older people who lived this life in rebellion and without Jesus come to Him at the last saying that as a child their parents and teachers had taught and showed them the way, and they had come to Jesus.

We can be sure that when godly parents live the Will of God the children can never get away from it. The things of God will live forever, and the things of this world are dying forever. Jesus lives that we may live also.

I had every opportunity in this world to have respect for my parents and older people because my Dad was already 71 years old when I was born into this world. At the age of 71 years, my Dad taught me to have a special respect for older people, and that I could benefit from the wisdom that they could share with me. I was told that I might not understand right away what I was being told, but the truth would come to me. Every day now after all these years (89 of them to be exact), the truth from the wisdom these older people shared with me pops up and I hear them say "I told you so." This gives me a special opportunity to make decisions that are right for me. This gives me the benefit of years of experience in what is right and wrong when I am called upon to make decisions that will affect my life here and also the lives of others.

Every day I have had to say, "You are right Dad." And I know that my Dad spoke from experience that he had had and I learned from him and the other older people that I listened to. They would always tell me not to go there, because I made a mistake in that, and it wasn't in accordance with the teaching of the Bible. These people of wisdom would always tell me when they made a mistake, and when they made the right decision.

Now while we think about the words above I want to say this. My Dad was born in 1859. And I was born in 1930. That was when my Dad was 71 years old. At the date of this writing I am 89 years old. Add 89 to 71 and you have 160 years and counting. I can remember what my Dad said and it affects my life now. I have the benefit from 160 years of experience in this life so far, and it is determined by how I listened and how much I have remembered of the wisdom that God has given me through my Dad and the other wise older persons.

The saddest thing is that as a stranger in this foreign land so many people are missing the wisdom of God as they pass through this life. The first one that they miss is Jesus. For without Him you can do nothing. With Him all things are possible. He is the Word of God, and through Him comes all wisdom. It is through Him that you can honor your parents and older people making them a channel of wisdom to you. Remember this is God's work.

Chapter 13 – To Live in Respect for God

From this point on in this account of my experience here in this life, I will try to record the changes that have come about over the years I have lived in this life here. Respect for God is one of the main things that changed in the years of my life here. As a society for the past 80 years we have slowly but surely come to live without fear that we will do those things that are pleasing to God. Without this respect for God's will in and for our lives, we have drifted from God to a dangerous place, and must return if things are to be good for us.

This lack of respect comes in our attitude towards God in our life here in this world. To list some of the things that are notable are: God's day, God's house, His Will in general and for our self and others. Without His Will in our lives we cannot prosper in any way. We should never attempt to be satisfied in any way until we are in His Will for our lives. Respect for God comes when we have respect for that which belongs to Him. This world is His creation and He has paid for all that have fallen by sending His Son to die on the cross, so that we all benefit from it.

About 75 years ago, in 1943, as a boy 13 years old, my Dad died and as a boy who loved his Daddy I was devastated, and it looked like my world had come to an end. And it seemed that there was no hope for me. But from this experience I learned that God's will for me was a life filled with hope. I learned that there was hope when God's will was done in and for my life.

It was the day of my Dad's funeral that God spoke loud and clear. We had gathered in a little one-roomed country church, and as I sat wondering how I would be able to go on from there, God opened my eyes and ears. As I looked at the casket I thought that this would be the last time I would see my Dad, and I looked at the choir that was filled with people of the community, and saw my teacher and other important people in my life. I listened as they sang a song that gave me hope and has given me hope for 75 years now. That song was "In the Sweet By and By" and it went like this; "There's a land that is fairer than day, and by faith we can see it afar: For the Father waits over the way To prepare us a dwelling place there. In the sweet by and by, we shall meet on that beautiful shore. We shall sing on that beautiful shore...."

When God's will is done, life here is not all of it. In the song "The Sweet By and By" (the future) our bountiful Father has prepared a place that is brighter than day, more wonderful than this present life for us. A few years ago I found my great-grandmother's grave and on the grave marker was this inscription "This Happy Soul has Winged Her Way to that Pure Bright Eternal Day." She was buried in 1894 and we will meet in the future on that beautiful shore.

Now what I am trying to say is that we need to live with respect for what God wants in our lives. And if we miss this our loss is tremendous. When God's will is done in our life in this world we are definitely better off, but it is definitely better for us in the next world, or eternal life. Now the song just mentioned says that by faith we can see what God wants for us and act on that faith. To believe that we are born in sin and need to be born again is to ask Jesus to come into our life and save us. It is to be born into God's family. Therefore God becomes our bountiful Father and we treat Him as such. We live our life always looking to please Him by studying His word and talking with Him daily.

The house of God is one of the things we can see the lack of respect for God change in. The building where the church meets is a building. It is a place where God's children gather for His service and to worship Him and as such should be respected because it is called God's house and we expect to meet God there. To fail here shows lack of respect for God Himself.

When we are saved we belong to God, and have been bought with a price. Everything that belongs to God should be respected as such, and we know that when we respect what is His it pleases Him. And when He is pleased we are doing the right thing. Our bodies become the tabernacle of the Holy Spirit when we are saved. Because our bodies are the home of God in this life we are to treat our bodies as what they are, the house of God. Now when God lives in a house you can know it, and then treat it with respect because it is God's dwelling place. When God is there, wherever He is, we must respect Him as our Father. There is a lack of respect for God today because our society is turning away from God. God is not respected in the lives of people, because He doesn't dwell in their bodies. God is not respected in the church house because He doesn't dwell in the lives of the people in the church.

God is our bountiful Father, and we praise Him as such. As children of God we are to desire that everything we do praises Him as our Father. Every child should be able to praise their Father, and the child of God has a reason to praise their Father. He is worthy of their praise. Because we are able to pray; "Our Father which art in heaven, Hallowed be they name." (Matthew 6:9-13) He will answer our prayers, and our needs are met according to His will. We have our needs because we ask according to His will. Our lives should bring honor and praise to God. We have no reason to be ashamed of God. We are to be ready to give Him the glory for everything in our lives. We are to live with such respect for our Father that He will get credit for all the good that comes out of our living. When we labor for our food, clothing, and shelter, He should receive the honor and credit for providing it. When we sing, he should be held up and honored, and we are not singing to exalt self or put on a show, but humbly praise God for His abundant love for us.

Everything that we do should be done as unto the Lord. In that way God will get the credit for it all. When this is done our Father will get the credit and everyone will have an opportunity to come to know God as their bountiful Father.

We have a Father at home waiting and preparing for our homecoming; and Jesus said; if it wasn't so He would have told us (John 14:2). Our real life will start when we cease to be here. We are going home to wander no more. We will be there forever and all of our loved-ones will be there with us. Our Father is waiting and in charge of the preparations for this great day of our lives. Dear Friend, you don't want to miss this occasion. Be sure that you seriously check with Jesus for this appointment. It's a chance of a lifetime for you to know God as your Father. Believe me, it will happen.

Chapter 14 – Two Different Influences in this Life from Two Opposite Sides

From this time in this writing, we will account for two different influences that those who are children of God, by being born from above, will have to deal with while living in this world.

September 20, 1943, my Dad died and we had his funeral at the country church in the area where we lived. I remember as I pondered the experience that I was having; we had just viewed my Dad for the last time. I sat on the front pew thinking I would never see my Dad again, and how final death was. I wondered what hope we could have but to wind up like this. Now my family, my church, and my school teacher had taught me about God and His Son Jesus and how God loved me, but how did that fit in here. I was a 13 year old boy who knew he needed his Dad and now it seemed Dad was gone forever.

Now while I was weeping, trying to make sense of what was happening to me, a choir had assembled of people of the community, and they began to sing. I wiped the tears from my eyes and there was my teacher in the front row. They began to sing, "There's a land that is fairer than day, and by faith we can see it afar; for the Father waits over the way to prepare us a dwelling place there. In the sweet by and by, we shall meet on that beautiful shore...." And on.

Now it has been 75 years and my life has been influenced continually by the spiritual message in that song. Because this message lives in my heart through the presence of the Holy Spirit, I have been influenced by this message of hope beginning with my being born again (born into God's family). My life in this world as a pilgrim has a different experience as I allow myself to be influenced by God's word when it is used by the Holy Spirit because I sought direction.

Now my experience in this life is that there are different influences. One is for good and one for evil (one from heaven and one from hell). For someone who has not been born into God's family it is an aimless, dying, and tormented life. Those who die in their sin will never know that really they have nothing to live for.

God used that song along with other songs in that country church and the people to influence me as I would listen to His Word and follow His direction. I couldn't get away from the message that I could meet my Dad later on where God had prepared a place for us to meet. Now this changed things and I couldn't get away from knowing that I could see my Dad in a beautiful place where we could sing and praise our bountiful Father (now that's life). And I thought about this all the time and I was saved 11 months later. I asked Jesus to come into my life and He did. He came in and is still there today. All that I knew then was that I was comforted at a time when I was very disturbed. The experience continued to give meaning to what Dad had said that He would be going away. I learned later that Jesus said "In My Father's house are many mansions: if it were not so, I would have told you. I go to prepare a place for you. And if I go and prepare a place for you, I will come again, and receive you unto myself; that where I am, there ye may be also." (John 14:2-3 KJV) As I tried to sing the words of this song continually, the Holy Spirit (the Comforter) continued to convict me that I needed Jesus as my Saviour and Lord. In August of 1944 (eleven months later), I asked Jesus to come into my life and take over, and He did that very day.

For me this ended the idea that my Father was gone forever, and from that day on it was as if he still lived and was there all the time. It is that way still today. I still turn my mind back to the things he taught me to do, and I do them. My Daddy still lives and I will be with him some day.

It has been 75 years now since my Dad's funeral and how I was influenced by the message in that song. I think of the messages and things that have come along the way that have in a way influenced or tempted me in my journey in this life. Because of my new birth when I became a child of God I have been tempted or influenced from two different sides and have had to make a choice in every one of them. Many times I have made the wrong choice and have suffered the consequences for that choice. But Jesus has always been there to take me by the hand and lead me out of there. He is always there to help us when we call on Him. Many have yielded to the influence of evil and suffered for it. The best influence we can have is the influence of a Christian parent like I had in my parents. And I thank the Lord for the Christian people God gave me as an influence in my life. I have stumbled many times but their influence showed me the way back to the right way. I thank God for the Christian people of the community that influenced me as a little boy who needed salvation. And especially for those who sang the song at my Dad's funeral which would show me the way. Too many today have yielded to the influence of evil and need to turn to Jesus for life and life more abundantly.

68

Chapter 15 – How Our Society has been Influenced by the Needs of the Flesh

The needs of the flesh are legitimate needs, and we are warned to be careful here. As a pilgrim here in this life I have a body fit for this life, and I will have a different body when I go home to be with God in heaven. This is not the kind of body that I will have there. We are to be influenced by the scriptural (Christian) way to use and care for these bodies. Jesus and Christianity show us how. God's word and His people will show us how to care for and use our body here. We need to check to see what God's will is here, because the flesh is house for the spirit and can get in the way of the spirit. When we are saved our body becomes the tabernacle of the Holy Spirit, and we are to treat it as such. Because we are a spirit who has a body of clay we need to be careful here. Now remember this body of fleshly clay was not fitted for heaven.

Now mankind is a soul and is a God-breathed spirit, a living soul. God breathed into mankind and he became a living soul. Now man is a spiritual being and in this life he has to have a body. When God's will is done with the body we will be alright, but when the devil uses this body we are going to be in trouble.

Over the years 1944-2019, there has been a tremendous change in the attitude of our society in respect to the flesh of man and it has not been for the better. In 74 years our society has gradually allowed the flesh to demand priority, and this is not good.

Now the flesh has honorable needs that must be met, but with the understanding that man is a living soul who has a body. That means that it is not fitted for anything but to go back to the dust of the earth. Just a place for the spirit of man to live while here on the earth. For anyone to treat the body as if it is all that man is would be wrong in any sense. Again the need here is to not allow the enemy of God to use the body of mankind to influence (tempt) him to do what is not the will of God. There is a lot that could be said at this point, but the primary need of man is for him as a living soul (spirit).

The word human is a word that is used to describe man in the flesh, so we will use that word at this point. Humanism has been something that has grown over the years of my life, neglecting the spiritual needs of mankind. In Humanism the spiritual needs of man have been put on the back burner so to speak. And this is one of the things that we will address here.

When it comes to Humanism there is a fine line that we need to be careful with. God cares about the total need of mankind. Jesus fed the 5000 with bread and fishes and then had to correct the folk for coming after Him for their physical need only. He is the primary need of man, and unless this spiritual need is met mankind has accomplished nothing. Most of those who are involved in God's churches today become so preoccupied with the needs of the flesh that they fail to care for the needs of the soul. This neglect shows in our society today. We can feed the body until it is overfed, while the soul is malnourished. It is evident in our society today that we have failed here. In Humanism a society is cared for in such a way that they have physical health problems while they are in spiritual poverty, very malnourished. There is no profit when the primary needs of the soul are not met.

You can look at a society and know when the needs of the soul have been neglected. Humanism has affected a society when the works of the flesh become a problem. The works of the flesh are: "adultery, fornication, uncleanness, lasciviousness, idolatry, witchcraft, hatred, variance, emulations, wrath, strife, seditions, heresies, envying, murders, drunkenness, revellings, and such like" (Galatians 5:19-21 KJV). Those that do these things are not spiritually right with God.

When I was a boy 14 years old in 1944, I lived in a Christian community, went to a Christian church, and attended a Christian public school. I was saved when our school teacher carried us to the church that I attended in the community that was holding revival services. Thirty-six people were baptized; most of them were young people like me. In 1944 things were very hard economically and we weren't overfed or cared for in excess, but we had enough to get by. The most important thing was we weren't neglected spiritually. The preacher came out from the nearby town to make it possible for us to have the message of God in this Revival. I remember that he rode a horse out there most of the time. I was taught by my parents, my church, and school that my greatest and main need was spiritual. Because I lived in a Christian community, hard times were shared by loving neighbors and we had enough to survive. We were taught to work at an early age and better off by it. Humanism wasn't a problem then. Although the works of the flesh were present and around then, they weren't acceptable because our spiritual needs were met by our parents, the churches, and the school in our community. They had done their job of directing us to Jesus. Needless to say the works of evil were around and tempting on every hand.

The reason for anyone to attend and/or belong to a church changed over the years that I have been in this world. When I was a boy we went to church because we needed Jesus in our lives to make our lives what they should be. We went there because it was the House of God and the House of Prayer in the community. All this gradually changed as more emphasis was placed upon material things. More people went expecting to be blessed with material blessings. With this, greed grew and produced many of the works of the flesh that come from coveting, adultery, fornication, lasciviousness, idolatry, murder, divorce, drunkenness, and many other works of the flesh. The bad in this is that those who want stuff for nothing wax worse. They do not want to work for what they get. Coveting is a growing thing and is strictly not the will of God. Those that allow the flesh to work in their life will never be satisfied. There is nothing about this that will please God. This produces poverty, broken homes, abandoned children, fatherless children, gambling, stealing, robbery, etc. We had some of this when I was a boy 75 years ago, but at that time society condemned all of this and we were taught that this was not the will of God. Now we have changed to a society that has banned God and His Son from the public schools and many of our children are raised without a true education.

When I was a boy we had to work as children to help make our living. We were taught that work was God's way for us to earn what we needed in life and not to expect those who earn their way to pay our way. Working was the honorable way to make our living and it was God's way. When I was seventeen years old in 1947 I was in the Tennessee State Guard. Our chaplain, who was a Pastor, brought us a message and he spoke about why people turn away from God. This we will discuss in the next chapter.

Chapter 16 – Becoming a Perverse Society

When I was a boy 75 years ago, I became a member of the Armed Services called "The Tennessee Guard" at the age of 17. One night our chaplain, a local Pastor, had a service. The teaching about Godless communism in this great country was in a big way and we were being warned about the disaster continually. Our chaplain mentioned this as he announced his subject, "Why people turn their backs and leave God out of their lives."

At that time we as a country had spent four years on our knees and been blessed by God. He said God had been allowed to have control, and He was blessing our country spiritually as well as materially. And he said that our country would prosper greatly, and the world through our country would be blessed also. He said that our country would become a perverse nation, and destroy itself from within. He quoted the Word of God from Proverbs and other passages, and what Jesus said "Oh, faithless and perverse generation." (Matthew 17:17 KJV) His message was that because money would become the God of this country, she would leave God out and no longer being able to have faith in God would turn to godless communism. He said that America would elect godless leaders, and in so doing would destroy herself from within. He said that the main Russian leader at that time had said the same.

God's word, including Jesus, is not silent when it comes to being perverse, and according to God's will it is not good. A faithless society becomes perverse. To be faithless you can get the money to get dirt moving machinery to move mountains, and you do not have to have faith. But Jesus said that real faith moves mountains. Now I have watched America for the past 75 years gradually turn from faith in God to the money god and disaster. Because I had been taught about the destruction of godless communism while in public elementary school and church, I have not been able to get away from the message that I heard that night.

Everything that I have been involved with has been affected from that time until now. In fact eternity has been affected for me. Jesus said, "Without me you can do nothing." I don't know for sure but it looks like the devil is involved here, because when Jesus dealt with faithlessness and perverse conditions he dealt with the devil. After all, the devil is a pervert. He cannot create anything, but he can pervert anything good that God has made. So you see He can bring about the perverse condition of disaster. Now when it comes to Jesus, He is the Word of God in its purest form and the devil cannot confront God's word. So it looks like perversion is caused by the devil.

There are a lot of things that do not make any sense in this transition to perversion, and we will try to list some of them now. I am going to begin with different denominations of churches, of which when I was a boy were very few then. The only thing that mattered then was Jesus and faith in God. Now before we go any farther we need to suggest that a dictionary be used to be sure what the word pervert or perversion really means.

Our Lord left the church here when He went back to Heaven. Now Jesus is the head of these churches, but someone it seems has been influencing the churches and it looks like a pervert. This faithless perversion of our Lord's churches doesn't make any sense at all. What sense does it make for a Christian nation to elect to ban public prayer in public schools, where children are to be taught the truth? Now look at perverted education that never comes to knowledge of the truth. Now we have to look at the churches that produce perverse ideas that cause such things to happen. We have so many out there that some don't even know what they are. You can find a church out there that will go along with any need you have to change in your life, and you will not have to repent and have faith in Jesus. We even have nondenominational churches out there so that you can believe whatever you want and still be part of the group.

There are not many churches out there that stand with the church that Jesus left here to carry out His mission on this earth. He gave us the teaching of the Apostles (the Apostle's Doctrine) to go by in order to be a church that He left here to carry out His mission of teaching and seeking the Lost. To consider: Seek to fulfill the "Ten Commandments" and present Jesus who is a fulfillment of the commandments, to those who repent and come to Him for salvation. Jesus said that He was here to fulfill the Law, and not to be a destroyer of the Law. He said, "They have Moses and the prophets, and let them hear this and turn to Jesus for salvation." (Luke 16:29) There are many organized bodies of people that are not standing with the church that Jesus set up and left here to do His work of salvation. Sinners that do not like the Biblical church can easily find a group of people that will make them comfortable in their sin. But this will not do when it comes to the Lamb's Book of Life and Heaven. (Revelations 20:12) Remember, God is only pleased with Jesus and the church He left here to do His work of salvation. These groups have brought about the faithless and perverse generation that we see today. We need to turn to Jesus today because without Him we can do nothing.

The history of this great nation depends on Jesus. He is the center of it all. He was there when it all began, and will be there when it all ends.

All that have sought to leave Him out and ignore Him have failed, and all who have become so faithless and perverse will fail in every way. Not a good thing to try to forget or ignore Him, because without Him you can do nothing. Now remember that history is His story. And without Him we have no history.

Communism, Socialism, or any other society that tries to function without God will vanish from history. Now the sad thing about this all is that when anyone tries to live as though there is no God, they will die as though there is no God. Somehow I do not believe that the majority of Americans are guilty of electing to have a godless society, but I believe that it was because of neglect on the part of God's people in the past. And I pray for them very much.

Legitimate money represents a successful life and our country proceeds to spend money that it doesn't have and it's not right to spend money that doesn't belong to us. Who will have to pay the debt that a faithless and perverse society builds up? Only God knows and can do anything about it. Those of faith in this country are the ones that can pray that God will do something about it.

Part Two – The Two Worlds We Must Encounter Here

Chapter 17 – A Culture that Wanders Out of the Way of Understanding

The child of God who is a stranger here in this life must not be influenced by a society that strays away from the will of God. A society like this is prone to wander and ignore the only hope for them. Every society that has allowed itself to forget God and leave Him out has disappeared from history and no longer exists.

For me as a stranger who has passed through this world to this point with a real faith, the devil will make accusations. God will convict and forgive. The result can be a hindered relationship with God, or it can be a better relationship with God. To create a better relationship with God the Christian must seek the will of God and just get on God's side every time. Put God first in everything you do. The pilgrim as a stranger (the Christian) is at home when he or she is in a society that relates to, acts on the mind, character, or will, morally; a society that is ethical, righteous, noble, virtuous, that opposes immorality in applying conformity in a standard of what is good and right. Our nation has been and is still a society founded on Christian principals but it has in many ways veered off course here as have many other societies.

The remainder of this writing will be about how I have been affected by two worlds, this world as we know it (material, the flesh, humanity) and the spiritual world to come. Primarily I became a stranger here when I was born from Heaven (spiritually) and have been affected by both worlds for good and bad. While living in the flesh I have made many mistakes. The Word of God tells us plainly how God wills it to be. This tells me that I always have room to improve and to depend upon Jesus in everything that I encounter here in this world. Every day we need to remind ourselves how helpless we are without Him. And we need to totally depend on Him. I learned how easy it is to make mistakes when I made decisions on my own. I have made many mistakes this way. Always take time to check how God wants it to be before you act, and you will know how to act when you know how He wants it to be. This way I have learned how easy it is to know God is with me in what I am going to do. Dear One, when God is with you who can be against you?

This world will always have a different way or reason to act than the way God wants us to act. We have to know that Jesus is the only way that we are able to have God's will in our lives. The only hope is for us to accept Jesus (who is the way, the truth, and the life). God has given us Jesus. Come to Him. Apart from Jesus we are by nature a child of this world. We need to be born from Heaven, making that your new home and this world your natural home. By being born into this world we are sinners born of sinners in a sinful world. We are doomed and have no hope, and are in need of someone to save us from the penalty of sin which is death, Hell, and the grave. This all seems unfair, but this world is not supposed to be fair. This world has turned its back upon the One who made it. And the individual that is born here possesses the same nature that the world has. So the sinner hates God and God's Son because of that nature. Now the devil has stolen God's creation from Him when He persuaded mankind to come to him and follow him. Now the devil is prince of this world because mankind has made him that. So God has said loud and clear that He will give man another chance.

The Holy Spirit began to impress on me the importance of my spiritual needs.

This all began in 1943 when I was 13 years old. I had a sister and two brothers that were younger than me. At my Dad's funeral I was devastated that I had come to the end of my dependence on my Dad and wondered what I would do. The choir began to sing "There's a Land that is Fairer than Day, And by Faith we can see it Afar, For the Father waits over the Way, To Prepare us a Dwelling Place There."

God sent His Only Son to bring Salvation to a lost world. Jesus came as the Christ, to save the world and this is what we were taught when it comes to the purpose of Jesus as God's Son here.

Back in the early Thirties and the Forties we saw our country and world turn to God and experience God's blessings abundantly. The Revival that this country experienced in 1943-1947 was a true revival in that many people met and accepted the Savior of their soul and lives. Since that day our great country has slowly and surely turned their back on God and become as Jesus said "lukewarm" (Revelations 3:16), compromising with the world and failing to live for God.

In those days we had circuit riding preachers that rode their horses into our communities preaching the Gospel of Salvation to all that would listen and heed their words. Our community had two primitive church buildings in it that were used by these preachers for meetings and church services. When there was not a building available, the people in that community would build a brush arbor. This was done by cutting poles and using brush to form a shelter. This brush arbor is illustrated below.

A "Brush Arbor" was built of poles and brush. Trees and brush were used to build a shelter where the services were to be held. Large logs were cut and used to hold large planks to make the seating for the people. They would go to the saw mill and get sawdust to put on the floor of these shelters. Many of the churches that exist today started as brush arbors. These faithful preachers followed their Lord in the spreading of the Gospel of Salvation.

It was 1943 when the Spirit of God began to impress upon me the need of spiritual things in my life. The presence of the Spirit was there every day to remind me of my needs there. God used my Dad's departure to lead me to Him and my salvation. And I learned the most important lesson of my life that there is something more important than this present world for me. That lesson is my spiritual needs are to be primary in this life and this lesson I have never been able to forget. Out of this comes the lesson that without Jesus in life I cannot accomplish anything. To leave Him out I will fail. Without Him I would not be saved, and without Him I cannot accomplish anything successfully.

My wife and I have always lived with the truth that without putting Jesus and His purpose for our lives first, we are missing the opportunity to have success and happiness in our lives. We have peace in our lives when we let Him tell us how it should be done.

When we want Jesus to be Lord of our lives, it is right for us to ask Him to direct us in everything we want to do, to ask Him what His will is. How can God direct our activities if we forget Him in what we do? God is a wonderful God. He will always let us know how it ought to be when we really ask Him. That brings us to the question of how God is able to let us know what His will is. The Word of God is the Sword of the Spirit. (Ephesians 6:13) Now this tells us that God's word is the way

He speaks to us, and Dear Friend, we need to listen. When we read the Bible do we listen to what God is telling us?

Now the Bible is a love letter from Heaven, and is to those who are saved, to those who are His children. Because it is a spiritual thing, the Holy Spirit is the way we can hear and heed it. And the saved are on God's side. They are able to hear and understand it.

Chapter 18 – The Convicting Power of The Holy Spirit

It is the work of God to convict, John 6:44-65. Conviction here means to have a strong belief or persuasion. God is a triune God, God the Father, God the Son, and God the Holy Spirit. All three offices through which God works are involved at all times, in the creation, in the salvation of the lost, and in the church and Christianity. See John 16:7-11. When Jesus paid for our sin on Calvary, He paid for salvation in our lives here on this earth. This makes it possible for God's will to be in our living here and now.

Before I was saved I felt like somebody was watching me at all times, and I thought it was my Dad. That may be true, but there was more to it than that. As I began to put things together I realized that it was the convicting power of God. It was the still small voice that I was hearing. God has to make it possible for us to come to Jesus for salvation, and it is the power of the Holy Spirit. It was that spirit that began to deal with me after I was saved.

I experienced the conviction of one who is lost (unsaved). While under conviction here, I had trouble knowing really what was wrong in my life. The only thing that I could do was continue trying to find the answer to what was going on with me. This is the answer I found when I was in revival at the church and the preacher made the statement that if you are convicted that you are lost, and must turn to Jesus for salvation. He will come into your life and you will be saved. This I did as I asked Jesus to take over in my life and He did.

Now when I was saved that was when my problems really started because I was born from Heaven, born from above. That made me a future citizen of Heaven. I became aware of two different worlds. I became aware that my friends (some of them) didn't see as I did. I became more aware of right and wrong in my living day by day. I was saved when I was 14 years old, and this made my 15th year a hard one because many of the things that I was tempted to do were wrong. And going along with some of the things my friends were doing got me in trouble. I would feel bad about myself and it seemed that the Lord would take me by the hand and say "come on, get away from this."

As a teenager of 15 to 17, I grew more spiritually by temptation because I was sensitive to "that still small voice" of God, the Holy Spirit. I learned that being born again made a difference in how I would live here in this world. Thank God He is still there and makes a difference in where I go and what I do in this world. Because I am still in this world and have to live among people who don't know Jesus personally, I have to deal with temptation. I have to be sensitive to the Holy Spirit and tell Satan to get behind me, that Jesus is my Lord.

Be assured that I have nothing more to brag about but my Lord and Saviour Jesus who is able to take care of me. And He will deliver me, and take care of me. He has so many times took me by the hand and said "come on," and led me out of things that I had gotten myself into. I will follow Him all the way. By doing this He has kept me from so many things that would have hurt me and others. He has kept me from being destroyed so many times, and all I can do is to praise Him for it today. It has been 74 years of knowing Jesus. Every day of these 74 years I have come to know my Saviour better and every day I have come to love Him more.

Every day I have come to know that this world is built around Him, and that there would be no history, no date, no time, and no living if it wasn't for Him. Therefore I have chosen to build my life around Him. Now I have already learned that I cannot do anything without Him but I know that He can do all that it takes. So precious Jesus here I am. Take me now and make me what I ought to be.

Chapter 19-The Maple Grove Schoolhouse – Heart of the Maple Grove Community

As a boy 81 years ago, this is what I remember the schoolhouse to look like. This is where most of the social functions were carried out in the community.

I was seven years old in 1937 when I started to school in the first grade. I still remember the things I learned there and the wonderful teachers I had. The parents would work together to assist in the education of their children. This was the meeting place for many functions of the community. The Maple Grove schoolhouse was truly the heart of the community in those days.

The education of the children was carried out here, and this was done in a very special way. I learned things there that children do not learn in school today. The things that I learned I still use today. I learned how to replace a broken window glass, how to get up and go to school early and build fires for the heat in the winter, and most of all how to be a responsible person.

The Home Demonstration Club would meet here when there wasn't a home for them to meet in. The County Agent would meet here with the Four-H Club, and there were other activities like showing a film. I remember the Christmas parties, and other special day parties.

The Mothers would help with the hot lunch program. Each mother would sign up for a week to help the cook with those meals. The men would cut the wood for the winter heating and pile it in the woodpile at the end of the schoolhouse. The parents of the community would work together for needs in and around the schoolhouse.

After 81 years I still benefit from what I was taught there. Many things were taught by word and by practice. We were taught about "The Faith of our Fathers" loud and clear at Thanksgiving and all the year long. We were taught that our Christian fathers came here to be able to worship freely (from state or any other organization). This was taught perfectly well on Thanksgiving Day. They made sure that the Christian parents were teaching the children about our pilgrim fathers who couldn't find any other place where they were able to follow and worship Jesus other than America. They had come to America to face all the hardships and opposition to be able to worship freely. Now the rest of the story is that our country became a Christian nation by their coming here.

Now for me Thanksgiving was the most important time of the year. Because at that time, 81 years ago, everyone in the Maple Grove Community identified with the Pilgrim Fathers in one way or another. They were all farmers of some sort. And that is what Thanksgiving is all about. Our pilgrim fathers had worked in their fields to have provisions for the winter, and God had given it to them. This was the time to thank Him for all that He had provided.

The school was located in the center of the community and we walked to the school every day and in all kinds of weather. Very few times anyone would have a ride. Wagons and buggies were the main mode of transportation with a car or a truck every now and then. We would be coming from all directions to the school and by the time we got to school the road would be full. The older kids would be responsible for the little ones. If you were the oldest in the family you took care of the little ones. It didn't matter whose little one it was. The older kids took care of them all. If the little ones fell in the mud, lost a book, or anything happened to them, the older ones would correct the small ones and keep them secure all the way or the older ones would answer for what had happened.

If the church had morning revivals up the road half a mile, one of the teachers would carry the older ones who wanted to go and other teachers kept the others at school. I was saved when we went to the revival one morning in August 1944. I have thanked the teachers for 74 years now for carrying us to the revival in August that morning in 1944.

I had a good start and I am still feasting off the start they gave me. We looked at our teachers as school moms. Truly they were our school mothers. They had chores for us to do around the school and grounds. There were fires to build in the morning, floors to sweep, kindling and wood to get in at night and the flag to put up or bring in at night. Our teachers had to manage this and they did a good job. Every evening in the winter the teacher would appoint two students to go gather sticks from the fence row or thicket for building fires. They would have two students to take down the flag in the evening. Two students were responsible for getting in wood for the fires in the morning.

In the morning they would lead us in a devotional by Bible reading, saying the Lord's Prayer, and pledging allegiance to the flag. They were really our school Moms when using that peach tree limb. They did a good job keeping us in line. I still thank the Lord for those teachers.

About the Author

Ben Frank Wood Jr., aka Bro. Ben, is a retired Baptist pastor. He has lived his life to simply represent his Lord and Savior Jesus Christ. After a lifetime of pastoring churches, building houses and cabinets, and teaching Building Trades and Drafting to high school students, he now spends his days growing tomatoes and visiting with his friends and family. He leads a small group, Blessed Assurance Bible Study, who meet in his garage/study on a weekly basis. His desire is to spread the word of God's saving power. He is preparing for that marvelous day when his work here is done and he can join his precious Peggy with their Lord for eternity.

Connect with Ben Frank Wood Jr. at bwoodtn@att.net.

Made in the USA
Columbia, SC
24 February 2025

54264843R00064